First published 1983

Macdonald & Co
(Publishers) Ltd
Maxwell House
Worship Street
London EC2A 2EN

© Macdonald & Co
(Publishers) Ltd 1983

ISBN 0 356 07536 2
(cased edition)
ISBN 0 356 07530 3
(limp edition)

Made and printed by
Purnell and Sons
(Book Production) Ltd
Paulton, England
Member of BPCC plc

Editor
Margaret Conroy

Designer
John Fitzmaurice

Production
Rosemary Bishop

Picture research
Caroline Mitchell

Illustrators
Peter Dennis/Linda Rogers
Associates
David Eaton
Richard Hook/Temple Art
(cover)
Cynthia Pow

Consultant
Dr. Frank Tallett
Lecturer in History
University of Reading

everyday life in the

Eighteenth
Century

Neil Grant

Macdonald Educational

The 18th century

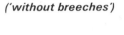

French revolutionaries

Two hundred years is not so very long ago. There are a few very old people alive now whose grandparents were born before 1800. The people and events in 18th-century novels are not so different that we cannot understand them.

In many ways the 18th century was a cautious age. Change was less obvious than it was in either the 17th or the 19th century.

Sans-culotte
('without breeches')

A popular picture of the age is of ladies and gentlemen in wigs and fine clothes sipping tea from porcelain cups and making witty conversation. Although such a scene is not entirely false, it is not a true picture of most people's lives. Change in society is always going on, and the 18th century is divided from us by two of the greatest changes (changes still going on) in history.

Nearly all European states were ruled by kings or queens. In a sense the monarch *was* the state, as the French king, Louis XIV, said. The monarch possessed very great powers, and subjects existed for the good of the state, not the other way around. The rights of other people depended mainly on their class – whether they were great nobles or poor peasants. By the end of the century, however, the French Revolution had shown the importance of people as individuals. Government, said the revolutionaries, depends on the people's agreement. The state is the nation – all the people – not just the king or the government.

The second great change which divides us from the 18th century was in methods of manufacturing goods. In the next century this was to alter the whole way of life of the people of western Europe, turning them from farmworkers and village craftsmen into factory workers and townsfolk. By 1800 the signs of this 'Industrial Revolution' could already be seen in parts of Europe.

Rich tea-drinkers

Coal miner

Russian peasants

Contents

The countries of Europe

In the 18th century Europe was divided into a number of states, much as it is today. But there were some differences. Neither Germany nor Italy was yet a united country; south-eastern Europe was still ruled by the Turks.

The population of Europe was very small by modern standards, but it was growing. France had about 17 million people in 1700 and about 26 million by 1789. Other countries grew even faster. This rise in population caused problems such as lack of food.

France was the greatest country in Europe although she was not as mighty as she had been in the 17th century. She was also influential. Most Europeans regarded her as the centre of civilization – the source of new fashions and new ideas.

Other countries were rising to challenge France, especially Prussia, Russia and Britain. Throughout the century the British were engaged in rivalry with the French for trade and colonies. The British led the way in the sensational economic changes known as the Industrial Revolution, which was to transform European life in the next century.

There were enormous differences in the way people lived in different parts of Europe, especially between east and west. Eastern Europe was poorer, and for most people life there changed very little in the course of the century.

▼ Catherine the Great, a German-born princess who became a great Russian empress (1762–96). Russia was the largest country in Europe, but in 1700 she seemed very remote and backward. During the 18th century Russia made many advances. For the first time, she joined the great powers of Europe on equal terms.

▶ The power of European states was spreading in other continents. This was only the start of the European hold over Asia and Africa which was to increase enormously in the 19th century.

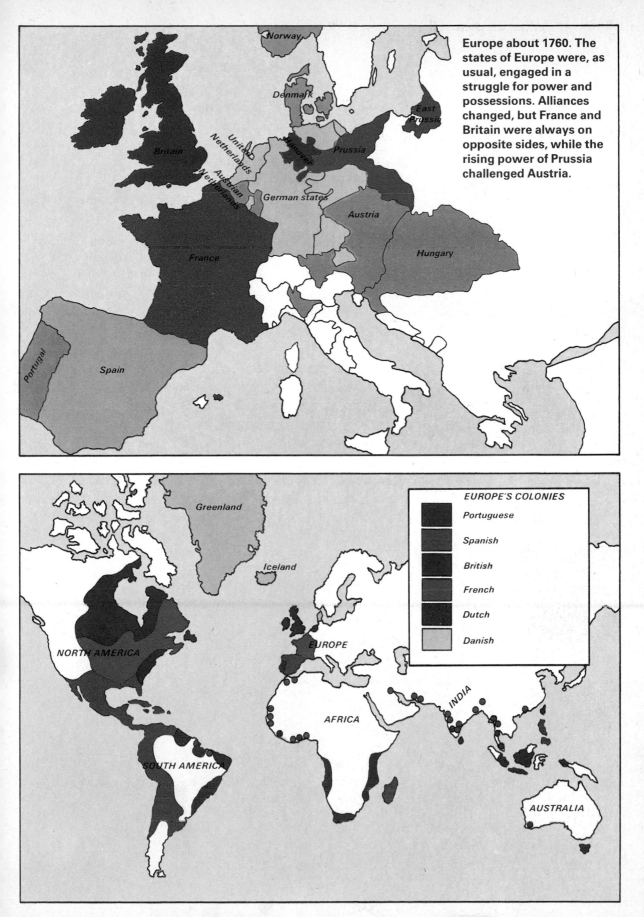

Europe about 1760. The states of Europe were, as usual, engaged in a struggle for power and possessions. Alliances changed, but France and Britain were always on opposite sides, while the rising power of Prussia challenged Austria.

Norway

Denmark

East Prussia

Britain

United Netherlands

Hanover

Prussia

Austrian Netherlands

German states

Austria

France

Hungary

Portugal

Spain

Greenland

Iceland

EUROPE'S COLONIES

Portuguese

Spanish

British

French

Dutch

Danish

NORTH AMERICA

EUROPE

INDIA

AFRICA

SOUTH AMERICA

AUSTRALIA

People and parish

Turf cover added so that wood smoulders rather than burns

Wood stacked in layers

▲ In many countries coal was becoming important, but most fuel was still provided by trees. Charcoal, needed in metal industries, was prepared in the forests.

Society in 18th-century Europe was divided into local groups or organizations, such as a parish or manor in the countryside, or a tradesmen's guild in the town. To a great extent these groups looked after themselves. Most food and clothing was produced in the neighbourhood. Criminals were sentenced by local courts, which also dealt with most forms of taxation and social services.

When people met at the inn or in church, they talked mainly about home affairs. They knew very little of what was happening in the capital city or even in the next county. When a beggar from Riom in the Auvergne (France) arrived at Coupière, less than thirty kilometres away, the local people could not understand his strange dialect.

Those who were not trained in some craft or profession often had no regular job. A man might be a fisherman in one season, a farm worker in another, a peddlar in a third. Although there were merchants, craftsmen, fishermen and so on, agriculture was by far the most common occupation.

The largest group of the population were peasants – people who worked on the land. Some rented their own patch. Others had no property and worked for wages. Some were serfs, which meant they were owned by a landlord who held extraordinary power over them. In most countries serfdom was fading away but in Russia it was actually increasing.

Most people in the 18th century lived close to nature. Everyone in the village helped with the harvest. If the autumn was wet, the harvest was poor and they would be hungry that winter. Heavy rains brought floods; a cold winter meant many deaths.

11

Social class

In 18th century society everyone knew his or her position, or, as we might say, class. Peasant or nobleman, you were born into a certain class and it was not easy to move out of it – practically impossible if (for example) you were a Russian serf. The social orders were clearly defined, almost as clearly as ranks in the army. But there was no promotion.

Hardly anyone questioned this system, which was supported by the teachings of religion. It seemed right and natural that some people were 'better' than others. The social order was held together by ancient custom. Each group had certain rights and duties which tied its members to the groups above and below them in the social scale. There was no basic

Upper classes

Wealthy merchant and his family, with pageboy

People often wished or pretended that their station was a higher one. In Smollett's novel, *The Adventures of Roderick Random* (1748), a woman travelling in a public wagon explains that she is taking this vulgar transport because her personal carriage has not turned up. She keeps looking for it on the road behind. Gradually we realize she has no private carriage, though she wants people to think she has.

'class conflict' between workers and bosses.

As time went by it became easier for people to rise in the world because of their wealth. Other economic changes were beginning to make nonsense of the old social customs. All the same, no one foresaw the destruction of the social order, not even the leaders of the French Revolution who did most to cause it.

Acceptance of the social order did not mean that everyone lived at peace with his or her neighbour. Riots and revolts were exceedingly common. Rampaging crowds of peasants invaded several Italian cities. The Ukraine (Russia) in the 1730s was in a state of almost permanent civil war.

But these riots were not directed against the social order. They were usually acts of desperation. The population was growing, but food and jobs did not increase. The result was famine and riot.

Most people believed in a social 'order': each individual had his or her proper station in life. A person's class was indicated by his or her clothes and way of life.

Soldiers

Farm workers

Peasants

Land and buildings

In the 18th century property was power. The land-owning classes, or nobility, were, with the monarch, the leaders of society.

In a country like France or Poland the nobility were, in general, an obstacle in the way of national prosperity and progress. The Polish nobles fought constantly among themselves. The French nobility lived in idle luxury, paying few taxes and wasting a fortune at court. In England, however, they were fewer, much richer, and more interested in their country estates.

Besides the great palaces and villas of the very rich, 18th-century architects designed excellent houses for the wealthy middle class. Edinburgh's New Town displays the solid but graceful housing built for prosperous town-dwellers. With its residential squares and crescents, it is an example of fine planning.

At the other end of the social scale, the poor often lived in houses that were little better than mud huts, with turf for a roof and bare earth for a floor. Some peasants were luckier, and by the end of the century cottages built of stone or brick were more common.

▶ The Zwinger Palace in Dresden (Germany) was built in 1710–20 for the ruler of Saxony. It is an early example of the extravagantly decorative Rococo style of the 18th century.

▲ During the later 18th century, Edinburgh earned its nickname, 'the Athens of the North', thanks mainly to its writers, philosophers and artists. The Old Town was a maze of narrow, winding and dirty streets but by 1800 the grand layout of the New Town was taking shape.

◀ Backs of the stately houses of Dutch merchants in Amsterdam. At the front is the street and another canal. The main rooms are on the first floor with steps leading from the street up to the front door.

▼ The home of a poor peasant family. Its one or two squalid rooms might house a large family plus chickens and goats.

Women and the family

▲ In poetry a milkmaid is usually a jolly lass, but carrying wooden pails slung from a yoke is hard work. Milk was not pasteurized, but still less dangerous than drinking water.

Almost everyone in the 18th century married, if they could, and had children. The family was more important than the individual person. Marriages were often arranged to add to the family fortunes.

It was especially important for a woman to marry. Single women were often treated as worthless members of society, who had failed to carry out women's 'natural duty' to produce children and run a household.

In most cases, the man ruled the family. Women did what their husbands told them. They had few rights as individuals: anything they owned on marriage became automatically their husbands' property. An English judge said it was legal for a man to beat his wife as long as he used a small stick!

Among poor people, too, the family was vital, because everyone who was able had to contribute to the family income. The wages of a farm worker were often not enough to keep his family. Wives and children had to earn something too. For women of the richer classes, there were simply no acceptable jobs except those of wife and mother. But poorer women sometimes worked in all kinds of occupations, even mining and road-building.

▲ In some parts of Europe, like the plains of Russia, even woòd was scarce. Fuel could be bought from travelling wood-sellers.

◄ Many families have left attractive records of themselves thanks to the fashion for family portraits.

Chambermaid

Lady's maid

Valet

Cook

Footman

Butler

Nursery maid

Washerwoman

▲ Women of the richer classes were not necessarily idle, since they were in charge of the household. A horde of servants had to be supervised – in kitchen, bedchamber, garden, orchard, dairy and so on. Visiting, letter-writing, embroidery and music-making occupied spare hours.

Children

Our ancestors' attitude to children seems shocking. As a rule, children were treated simply as small and annoying adults. Many mothers (especially upper-class mothers) showed little obvious affection for their babies. If they could afford it, they hired other women to nurse them.

There may have been a reason for this coolness. Babies and young children often died: if you had four children, you would be lucky to see more than one grow up. The coolness of parental love may have been a way of making it possible for people to endure the death of so many of their children. The life of children was much harder than now and cruelty and neglect were probably more common.

During the century the dreadful death rate of children went down, and attitudes towards children also changed. Mothers showed more love for their babies and dressed them in sensible, loose clothes – not simply smaller versions of grown-up clothing. The first shops specially for children were opened. More toys and books were made for them. Many parents rejected fairy stories as being unsuitable nonsense, and gave their children factual works to read instead.

But such changes were limited to certain families – mainly upper- or middle-class people in some western European countries. An English traveller in Spain wrote, in surprise,

▲ A child's game. The bobbin is thrown into the air and then caught again, on the string.

▼Dolls date back to prehistoric times, but the jigsaw puzzle was a new invention. Jigsaws were often made from maps, as people believed play should be educational or useful, if possible. Someone even invented a seesaw which drove a mechanical pump.

that it was nearly impossible to buy toys or books for children.

In most working families children became wage earners as soon as possible. Even at four or five, a child could earn a few pence by keeping birds off the crops. There was nothing new in children working, although the attempt by the government of Saxony (Germany) to make child labour *compulsory* was taking things too far even for people of the 18th century!

▲ Children of the poorer classes began to earn their living almost as soon as they could walk. Fairly simple tasks like spinning hemp ropes in a 'rope walk' could be done by quite young children, although some strength was needed to turn the spinning wheel.

► People who could afford them wore elaborate clothes in the 18th century and dressed their children in the same way. The well-to-do Graham family (painted by the Englishman William Hogarth in 1742) have pets (cat and canary) and a baby carriage which has a moving wooden bird on the top.

Education

▼ A tailor and his apprentices. All craftsmen learned their trade by apprenticeship – working for, and learning from, a trained craftsman, in whose house they lived. The system worked well – if the master was a decent man.

Intelligent people realized that education for all young children was a good idea. But by 1800 it existed nowhere except Austria, Prussia and Scotland. Children of the peasants and the poor – the great majority – seldom went to school and could not read.

Education made few advances in the 18th century. The main subjects were Latin, Greek and religious studies though modern subjects (geography, maths, modern languages) were gaining ground. Teaching was dominated by the Church, especially in Catholic countries. Otherwise teachers were few in number and badly paid, though the first teacher training colleges were founded.

Educational reform was in the air, but its practical results were small. Jean Jacques Rousseau believed that a child should be educated as a person, not just for a profession such as the Law or the Church. He thought girls should be educated too (very few were) though mainly in practical subjects. Other reformers urged more training for an occupation, fewer beatings and less Latin!

The great intellectual movement of the 18th century was known as the Enlightenment. It emphasized the value of reason and gave birth to the theories of future reformers, and involved people entirely outside the schools and universities.

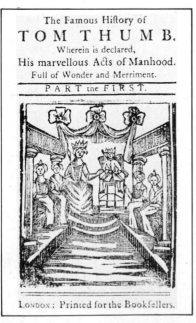

The Famous History of
T O M T H U M B.
Wherein is declared,
His marvellous Acts of Manhood.
Full of Wonder and Merriment.
PART the FIRST.

LONDON: Printed for the Bookfellers.

▲ Title page of a children's book.

▲ At any time people probably learn more from each other than from lessons or lectures. At home, mothers taught their children and older children taught their younger brothers and sisters.

Schools varied enormously. Teachers in general had a low position in society. There was much parrot learning and copying verses on slates (paper was expensive). In many schools, the best remedy for pupils' errors was believed to be a beating.

▶ With a few exceptions, like Leyden, Edinburgh, Gottingen and Halle, universities made little progress in the 18th century. They were dominated by the clergy and even lectures were given in Latin. As can be seen here, rich students were more inclined to enjoy themselves than to study.

Gardens and plants

A garden is an artificial thing. If it were 'natural' it would be full of weeds. The gardens of the great palaces and country houses of the 18th century were planned like a diagram, with ponds, fountains, lawns and terraces laid out in a regular design.

Later in the century it became fashionable to have what was called an 'English' garden. This would be planned no less carefully, but was wilder in appearance, with shrubs and trees growing in a more natural landscape. Some people even put in dead trees to help the 'natural' appearance.

Less wealthy people depended on their gardens and orchards more for food than decoration. Even in the towns, there was often a pig or some chickens in the backyard.

Some cities had public parks and pleasure gardens like the famous Vauxhall Gardens in London (admission one shilling, or 5p). Visitors could watch the aristocracy having a picnic – or they might be mugged by a ruffian. There was an orchestra, pantomimes and firework displays. At Ranelagh Gardens (London), the eight-year-old Mozart gave a recital in 1764, playing his own compositions on the harpsichord.

Botanical gardens – museums of living plants – were created in some cities. The experiments carried out at some of them led to better crops for farmers.

Magnolia

▲ Many new flowers and plants were brought back by travellers from distant places in the Far East, South Africa and the Americas.

► Scientific progress is often a matter of classification and measurement, not brilliant new ideas. Botany became a recognized subject thanks to the classification of plants by the Swedish botanist, Linnaeus.

Azalea

Camellia

► The gardens at Stourhead (England), one of the earliest examples (1741) of 'landscape' gardening.

◄ The Petit Trianon at the palace of Versailles, near Paris. The formal style of the garden was in keeping with the rest of the gardens at Versailles, which had been designed by Le Nôtre in the 17th century.

Farming

Turnip

Potatoes

Maize

▲ Many new crops were grown more widely in the 18th century.

▼ Thomas Coke (on the left) with his Southdown sheep. Coke was one of the leaders of the 'Agricultural Revolution'. He increased the value of his Norfolk estate ten-fold by using better farming methods.

New developments in agriculture in the 18th century made it an important period in the history of farming. But agricultural methods varied enormously. Most of eastern Europe was divided into huge estates which were worked by serfs. In France and Italy much of the land was held by peasants in tiny plots.

Throughout western Europe the ancient open-field system was still going strong. Peasants grew crops on their own small strips, scattered around huge fields, and grazed their animals on the common pasture. This was not a very efficient system.

The growing population required more food, which meant more efficient farming was necessary. In most countries change did not come fast enough, but in England especially, combining strips to make fields and pastures enclosed by fences became more common. This led to better farming, but forced many smallholders to sell up and become labourers.

Another wasteful aspect of the old system was that fields lay fallow every third year, so only two-thirds of farmland was in use. Farmers in Norfolk and elsewhere devised a new system of crop rotation. They grew new crops like turnips and clover in the third year and so kept the land permanently productive.

▲ Experiments in breeding led to better livestock, like this Lincolnshire bull (painted by George Stubbs). John Andrews, a farm worker, developed a more productive strain of barley.

▼ Jethro Tull's seed drill planted seeds in orderly rows, allowing a plough or hoe to pass between them. Previously, seed was scattered by hand, which wasted seed and made hoeing impossible.

Seed hopper

Seed falls out through funnel into furrow made by sheat

Sheat

Harrow to cover seeds

Clothes and fashion

In many places laws restricted the clothes a person might wear. People were expected to dress according to their social station, and though in practice such rules were seldom enforced, they were absurdly strict in theory. In Frankfurt (Germany) the citizens were divided into five classes, each distinguished by their dress.

Fashion in clothes is often ridiculous. The 18th century was set apart by its beautiful art, architecture and design, but this good taste did not extend to fashion. The enormously wide skirts, worn by society ladies and held in position by a frame, forced them to shuffle through doors sideways.

Some young men also adopted outrageous clothes, with vividly striped waistcoats and breeches. In England they were called 'Macaronis', perhaps because the style began in Italy.

The Macaronis painted their faces, like women. The use of make-up containing arsenic, mercury and white lead had terrible results – ruining the skin, making the hair fall out, causing infection, even death. Belonging to the upper classes had some disadvantages: peasant women, naturally, could not afford such dangerous adornments.

*Riding dress
1778*

*Riding dress with
redingote greatcoat
1786*

*Lady's wig
(built up on pad)
about 1780*

*Campaign wig
1741*

*Hedgehog style
1785*

*Full toupée
with curls
1789*

*Ramillies wig
1780*

Wigs, powdered white, were worn by both men and women who could afford them. Amazingly elaborate hair arrangements were worn (see the ship head-dress opposite). Wigs tended to be smaller as time passed and fashions became plainer and simpler. In revolutionary France wigs were officially abolished in 1795.

Agricultural worker's smock

Gentleman's clothing about 1720

Street dress 1780-95

Of course, the majority of people were not much affected by changing fashions. Peasants and country folk usually wore a simple smock and wooden clogs. One new item of clothing that made its appearance was trousers, although loose pantaloons were worn earlier in Italy. Trousers were first worn by sailors and farm workers; the gentry did not take to them until the 19th century.

Dress 1799

Street seller's clothing

ady's wig
out 1780

Open gown 1780

There was more ceremony and display in ordinary life in the 18th century, and personal dress and decoration were signs of social position. Only 'gentlemen' wore swords. When an English lord was hanged for murder, he was entitled to a silk rope. The style of a man's wig or the 'beauty patches' stuck on a lady's face could indicate rank, age, or even political sympathy.

Boot 1720

Lady's damask shoe 1785

Peasant's clog

Books and reading matter

▲ Voltaire was one of the leading *philosophes*, French intellectuals who criticized 18th-century society. He was among the contributors to Diderot's *Encyclopédie*. This was the century's greatest achievement in book publishing and tried to include all human knowledge.

▼ Newspapers were common by the end of the century. This picture of a Paris newspaper seller appeared in a magazine in January 1791.

'Formerly', wrote a German journalist in 1806, 'reading was the affair of the scholar and truly cultivated man. Now it is a general habit, even of the lower classes . . . '

The amount of printed paper of various kinds – books, newspapers, periodicals – increased enormously during the 18th century. Writers were no longer dependent on support from aristocratic patrons. Plays and novels with a realistic background, about middle-class people, became very popular; but there was also a huge output of cheap books for people of little education – such as craftsmen and peasants (if they could read).

The most dramatic growth in journalism occurred towards the end of the century. Only 35 newspapers and periodicals were published regularly in Paris in 1769; ten years later there were 169. One paper in Holland, a small country, sold 24,000 copies of each issue.

Most newspapers and periodicals, especially if their contents were political, were under strong government influence. The freedom of the press hardly existed in most countries, and editors who offended the government were likely to end up in prison. Some papers were printed in secret, or outside the country in which they were sold.

In spite of this, the 18th-century journalists produced a rich crop of political and social satire, and a growing number of people were able earn their living as professional writers.

▲ In spite of the lack of press freedom in many countries, the 18th century produced a rich crop of satirists, who attacked ideas, individuals or groups. Political cartoonists were especially savage. This is James Gillray's sketch of a political mob. Politicians and voters were equally corrupt.

► Books were expensive, but circulating libraries made them more easily available, for a small fee. A few scholarly libraries, like the British Museum, were open to the public.

The growth of towns

Towns and cities had a special importance. They were the places where change began, where new ideas were published – and where rebellions started.

Cities and towns in the 18th century were small by modern standards, but in western Europe they were growing rapidly. Increasing trade caused the growth of Atlantic ports like Nantes or Liverpool. In the course of the century, Liverpool changed from a sleepy fishing port to a large commercial city, chiefly from the profits of the slave trade.

European towns often enjoyed a high degree of independence from government. The imperial cities of Germany were, in fact, independent states, but even in nations like France, Spain or England many towns possessed self-government and even, in some cases, their own military defences. Towns were the places where rebellions started.

Because travel was so slow, even small towns acted as the 'capital' of their district, supplying all local needs. They had a character which has been partly lost since it became easy to order goods from a great city far away.

Although townspeople were a small minority of the population – roughly ten per cent on average – their importance was much greater. Country people often resented this fact.

As a rule the town government was dominated by a few rich merchants, who were becoming increasingly powerful in society as a whole and challenging the power of the land-owning nobility in some countries. The mass of the citizens – craftsmen, minor civil servants and the like – objected to this arrangement and sometimes rebelled against it. This was the age of the city mob. Since there was no regular police force, riots broke out easily.

The fast-growing towns swamped the small units into which society had been organized and the old customs and privileges which united it. Parish boundaries disappeared under new suburbs which helped to destroy the old society.

▲ A great deal of business was done by merchants and professional men over tea or coffee in the coffee houses of the cities.

Town life

There were more shops than ever before, selling a larger variety of goods. As towns grew in size, shops became more specialized and more widespread: no longer would you find all the butchers on the same street.

Robbery was common, and so was fraud. Such laws as there were to protect customers had little effect. In Paris, dishonest grocers mixed powdered dog dung into their pepper: wise customers insisted on having their pepper ground before their eyes. Strange things found their way into tea which, like coffee, was becoming very popular. In England, government duty (tax) made tea expensive, but you could sometimes buy it at a price less than the duty alone – because so much tea was smuggled into the country.

Shopkeepers wrapped goods, if at all, in any available paper. It is said that a shopper in Paris found his purchases had been wrapped in the king's marriage contract.

Though life in an 18th-century town would seem rowdy and disorganized to us, some improvements were being made. Houses were being numbered at last, so mail could be delivered more easily. There were traffic laws to reduce the chaos in the streets but, like most 18th-century laws, these were often disobeyed. More streets were paved, more were lit, more sewers were enclosed, and more water was carried in pipes, which thus reduced disease.

▼ Most 18th-century towns were noisy and smelly. Iron carriage wheels on cobblestones were just as noisy as motor vehicles. Few towns had proper sanitation, lighting or rubbish collection.

► An English brewery. Wine, beer and spirits were fairly cheap, and drunkenness was a growing problem.

▼ Social services were improving slowly. Some were run by private organizations. Early London fire brigades, for example, were formed by insurance societies. They would only put out a fire if the property were insured by their company, and because of open fireplaces, accidents were common. A few places, like the Bank of England, did, however, have central heating.

Entertainment

The circus became popular in the late 18th century. The main act was acrobatic horseback riding (by men and women riders) which is easier when the horse is galloping in a circle (or 'circus'). Circus performances took place mostly in specially designed buildings.

In earlier ages, people generally had less leisure time, and their entertainments were more often 'home-made'. For instance, most members of middle-class families in the 18th century could play a musical instrument.

However, the towns provided a growing variety of entertainment for those who could afford it. The theatre flourished. But the plays written in this century, except for some good comedies, were less impressive than the beautiful theatres built for their performance.

The most striking theatrical development was the

popularity of opera. There were forty opera houses in the Papal States (Italy) alone. Instrumental music was almost as popular, and it was written by some of the greatest of European composers – J. S. Bach, Mozart and Handel.

Like opera, ballet was becoming more professional, and it produced its first internationally famous 'stars', like the French dancer, Gaetan Vestris. Women dancers were restricted by their long skirts and there was no point in clever footwork if the audience could not see your feet. Spectacular stage devices like the 'flying machines' which carried the dancer through the air added to the excitement.

For the mass of the people, entertainment usually took simple and crude forms. For example, the execution of criminals was a public spectacle which attracted huge crowds.

▼ Attitudes to insanity changed for the better in the 18th century. In 1766 Bedlam, the famous insane asylum in London, finally stopped its practice of admitting visitors (for a fee) who came just to laugh at the inmates.

► The improvement in roads, especially near towns, and the increasing use of carriages made it possible to take day trips into the countryside. Picnicking became popular but was not always peaceful!

Sports and games

Most of the games played today were also played in the 18th century, but in a form which we should not recognize. Football, for instance, often involved a whole village; the game ranged over a large area of ground, and could develop into a riot.

Various stick-and-ball games were also played. The English game of cricket received its first rules in 1744, and the Prince of Wales died after being struck by a cricket ball. The only form of tennis played was the kind now known as 'real' tennis, in an indoor court with various 'hazards'.

'Gentlemen' usually preferred the traditional, more military sports of hunting and racing. After a day at the races or in the hunting field, the upper classes might spend the evening gambling with cards, at which large fortunes were lost and won in an evening. Addicted gamblers had chamber pots built into the sideboard so they need not leave the room. The English Lord Sandwich gave his name to the snack he had brought to him rather than leave the card table to eat.

► The chief interest of the upper classes in most sports was in betting on the result. Gambling was widespread: in England it was almost a national disease. Roulette (right) was a French invention.

▼► Hunting was the main relaxation of the ruling classes. Many of Europe's royal palaces began as 'hunting lodges', the equivalent of the modern businessman's weekend cottage. The traditional quarry was deer, but as the sport was taken up by the middle classes, the fox became the chief object of 'the chase', especially in England.

▼ Horse-racing was a sport enjoyed by duke and peasant alike. In the excitement, spectators, many on horseback, would gallop up the course behind the race.

Religion

One sign of the decreasing power of religion in the 'age of reason' was that people no longer fought wars over it. Many educated people openly expressed doubts about the truth of Christianity, something they would not have felt (and certainly would not have admitted) in an earlier age. Voltaire, who launched fierce attacks on religion and the clergy, found an eager audience.

However, few people rejected religion altogether, and it remained the most powerful influence in the lives of many. Religious books sold in larger numbers than any others; thousands still flocked to pilgrim shrines; the churches were still full. In Catholic countries especially, religious feeling among ordinary people was intense. In general, both the Roman Catholic Church and Protestant state Churches supported and strengthened the traditional social order.

The basic strength of religion appeared in new Christian sects and movements. Methodism in England and Pietism in Germany stressed the importance of faith and feelings – rather than dry teachings – in religion.

In spite of the Enlightenment – and the broad-minded views of some rulers on this subject – religious freedom hardly existed. Intolerance was worst in eastern Europe: several Protestants were executed in a Polish town in 1719.

▼ Though many people took religion less seriously than their grandfathers did, nearly everyone had some kind of religious faith, however vague. Official religion and church-going helped to maintain the old 'order' of society, headed by the parson and the squire.

▲ Methodism came about as a reaction against the new belief in 'reason' and the lack of earnestness or inspiration in the Church of England. Its founder, John Wesley, travelled 40,000 kilometres preaching mainly to poor people. His powerful sermons and passionate hymns made many converts.

◄ The Jesuits had been the most powerful missionary force in the Roman Catholic Church since the 16th century. The Emperor Akbar of India (shown here) had long discussions with Jesuits to find out more about their beliefs. They encountered strong opposition in the 18th century, partly due to their dominant influence on education. In 1773 their Order was suppressed by the Pope, but the ban lasted only a few years.

39

Arts and crafts

The decorative arts were at their most elegant in the 18th century. The finest work of the silversmith or cabinetmaker was, of course, made for rich people. But there was some elegance and refinement to be seen in the homes of all but the very poor. The new habits of drinking tea and coffee encouraged progress in the pottery industry, and china plates and cups replaced the wood or pewter of earlier times.

True porcelain, a translucent (light passes through) form of pottery, had long been imported from China. In the 18th century, Europeans finally discovered how to make it themselves. Ordinary earthenware (non-translucent china) was also improved and sold to more and more households. In England, Josiah Wedgwood produced splendid pottery that was fairly cheap as well as elegant.

Style in art and design changed greatly in the course of the century, especially in the later years. The excavation of the ancient cities of Pompeii and Herculaneum led to a fashion for Classical (Greek and Roman) design. The elegant patterns of the Adam brothers in Britain from about 1760 were early examples of this 'Neo-Classical' style. The great Brandenburg Gate in Berlin was another. Oriental influence also appeared – for example, in Chippendale's designs for furniture.

Chippendale straight-backed chair

The 18th century was the last period in which most articles were made by hand, not by machines.

One style in furniture was named after Louis XV of France (1715–74) and was widely copied throughout Europe. It was light and delicate, and was often inlaid in fine patterns.

French gilded armchair, similar to one made for Marie Antoinette in 1788

French harpsichord 1786

German glass bell with silver handle

▲ Labour, even skilled labour, was cheap. Much time could therefore be spent on making and decorating glassware and pottery.

English (Worcester) porcelain 1770

▼ A blacksmith was important in village life. He shoed horses and made and repaired farm equipment and household goods such as candle holders and locks. But he also made finer and more decorative articles such as weather-vanes and fire irons.

Warfare

American French German

▲ Military uniforms were more colourful than practical, and battles were fought by traditional rules. An able general like Frederick the Great surprised his opponents by unusual tactics such as attacking up a hill.

▼ Noise, smoke and blood on a cramped naval gun deck.

In every century, Europeans have fought wars among themselves or against others, often over territory. The 18th century was no exception, yet it was a less violent period. Many wars were fought, but mostly by small armies, and they were less damaging than in earlier times.

Of course, there were exceptions. Poland disappeared altogether, divided up by greedy neighbours. In eastern Europe generally, wars were waged more fiercely than elsewhere.

Although the troops were mostly professionals, soldiers' and sailors' wages were low and not always promptly paid. Discipline was strict, enforced by savage floggings. Equipment was poor, or lacking altogether. Despite the invention of explosive shells and rapid-firing guns, there was little advance in weapons. Battles – on land or sea – could be fought and won with surprisingly few casualties.

Some kind of compulsory military service existed in most countries. But the real change in armies came with the troops of Revolutionary France. They were the first truly national army, with a general call-up of all eligible citizens. Thus war directly affected every family.

Perhaps the most important war for the future of the world was the American Revolution, an early example of a victory by a citizen army over regular troops. The democratic, republican form of government set up in the United States was an example to other countries, notably France, which had assisted the American revolutionaries against Britain.

Trade and colonies

International trade grew rapidly in the 18th century. By 1800 Britain had emerged as the strongest trading nation, thanks to its overseas colonies. (Some, like India and Canada, were seized from the French.) Britain's position was also due to its powerful navy and the low price of its products.

New ideas on economics were set forth by the *Physiocrats* in France, and by Adam Smith in his *Wealth of Nations* (1776). They attacked the old ideas that trade should be strictly controlled and protected by governments and that countries' import of goods should be kept to a minimum.

Large fortunes could be made quite easily in trade. A ship's

▼ For maritime nations, the most profitable trade was the 'triangular' trade – cheap trade goods (especially guns) from Europe to Africa; slaves from Africa to America; sugar and other colonial produce from the Americas back to Europe. The three legs of the voyage formed a triangle on the map.

▼ The trade in slaves, at its height in the 18th century, was one of the most evil episodes in all European history. Millions of innocent men, women and children were transported across the Atlantic in dreadful conditions. In one frightful incident, 122 Africans were thrown into the sea so that the shippers could collect the insurance. Some spoke out against the trade, but it continued as long as it remained profitable.

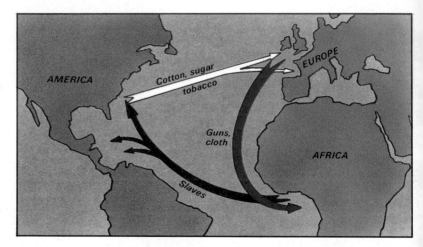

carpenter from Bristol saved up 15 pounds with which he bought sugar in the West Indies. Selling it in Bristol, he bought British goods like clothes and tools with the profits, and exchanged them for more sugar on his next voyage. He soon built up a business which, in his son's time, was valued at half a million pounds.

European governments valued colonies because they produced cheap raw materials and provided a market for manufactured goods. But colonies had other advantages for Europe. They provided an outlet for surplus population and, in time, they became new societies which were different in many ways from the society that gave birth to them. Disagreements between Britain and its North American colonies led to the foundation of the independent United States of America in 1776.

While the British lost old colonies in North America, they gained new ones in the Pacific. The first colony in Australia began at what is now Sydney, New South Wales, in 1788. The hard work of land-clearing and building was done by convicts.

45

Transport

Much the easiest way to get about was by water. It was cheaper for merchants in Brittany to trade with the West Indies than to trade with another part of France. Packhorses and wagons were slower and more expensive.

Inland water transport was improved by the construction of canals. An early example was the Canal du Midi in France, between the Bay of Biscay and the Mediterranean (completed 1681). In Britain, a large network of inland canals and navigable rivers was constructed in the late 18th century. The pioneer canal builder was the Duke of Bridgewater. His engineer, James Brindley, built a canal to carry coal from mines on the Duke's estate to the industrial city of Manchester.

Great improvements were made in road and bridge building in many countries in the late 18th century. By about 1780 a stage coach could rattle along at 15 kilometres per hour or more for long distances in countries like Austria, England and France, stopping only to pay tolls or to change the horses.

For ordinary people, travel was expensive, slow, uncomfortable and dangerous. A man about to make a long journey by coach was advised to make his will first!

▼ Road accidents were common long before there were motor vehicles. Roads were terrible: in Spain, until 1777, there were no roads fit for carriages except those leading to royal palaces. Arthur Young, travelling through England and France, found 'rocky lanes full of hugeous stones as big as one's horse, and abominable holes'.

▲ The first cast-iron bridge, at Coalbrookdale, England, was finished in 1779. It marked the end of the reign of stone and timber in bridge building.

▼ The engineering profession was born in the 18th century, and the first great engineering projects were the canals. Many were built to cross deep valleys on aqueducts and to pass through mountains in tunnels.

Travel and exploration

18th-century readers were very interested in travel books. Not only descriptions of their own country but also stories of journeys in strange places, such as Robinson Crusoe's desert island or the new lands of the Pacific, were very popular.

Educated people were becoming more interested in non-European cultures. They no longer lumped together all non-Christians as pagans or savages, and they were interested in other civilizations, like those of China and India, which were actually older than their own. Rousseau and others encouraged the yearning for a simpler kind of life, closer to Nature and free of the complexities of European civilization. The voyages of explorers, and their discovery of Tahiti and the Friendly Isles, produced some evidence in favour of the idea of happy islanders living in a Garden of Eden.

Long-distance sailing was assisted by the invention of the chronometer (a ship's clock). Previously it had been impossible to measure time accurately over a long period on a ship (where pendulum clocks were no good), and unless you can measure time, you cannot measure longitude (relative position east-west).

Explorers opened the way for missionaries and traders – and eventually soldiers and administrators. Until the 18th century only the Roman Catholic Church had sent missionaries to new lands in large numbers. Now, growing numbers of Protestant missionaries ventured into the forests and plains.

▶ The French explorer La Perouse (far right) with Louis XVI (second from right), planning La Perouse's expedition to the Pacific. He landed in Australia but the expedition spent a large part of the time (between 1786 and 1788) charting the Samoa group of islands.

▶ One reason for the advances made in geography in the 18th century was the growing interest in exploration. The Scot, Mungo Park (1771–1806), discovered the true course of the Niger River for the British African Association (forerunner of the Royal Geographical Society). Like later travellers, he found West African women helpful but also very curious about his colour and clothing.

◄ The travels of explorers put an end to many uncertainties. The voyages of Captain Cook should have ended the myth of a huge Southern Continent, though in fact it lingered on. Cook explored New Zealand where he met Maoris such as these. His reports led to the settlement of many areas by the British.

Doctors and scientists

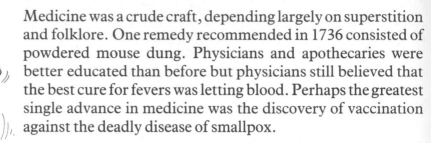

Medicine was a crude craft, depending largely on superstition and folklore. One remedy recommended in 1736 consisted of powdered mouse dung. Physicians and apothecaries were better educated than before but physicians still believed that the best cure for fevers was letting blood. Perhaps the greatest single advance in medicine was the discovery of vaccination against the deadly disease of smallpox.

Surgical knife

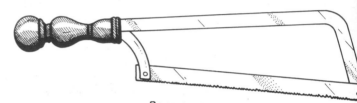

Bone saw

▲ Travelling dentists could often be found at fairs. They filled teeth but did not drill away rotten parts, so decay continued. The only real remedy for toothache was extraction.

People had a lot of trouble with their teeth. False teeth could be had, but they were used for appearance's sake only. An old lady at Louis XV's court used to put her teeth on the table while she ate.

Spectacles were also quite common. They were valued possessions and were often mentioned in 18th-century wills.

Dramatic progress in many scientific fields had begun in the 17th century and great advances continued. Linnaeus made botany and zoology systematic, and Lavoisier founded the modern science of chemistry.

In technology, the building of canals led to the new profession of civil engineer. James Watt invented a new type of steam engine which was to provide the power for the Industrial Revolution. Hundreds of useful tools and machines were invented.

▼ Antoine Lavoisier (1743–94) was the true founder of the modern science of chemistry. His work was important not for results alone but also for the precise methods he developed.

▼ Surgery without anaesthetics or antiseptics was crude and dangerous. Surgeons were practical men, and their instruments (left) looked like butchers' tools. But they were becoming more scientific, and learned their trade by dissecting corpses. Although no longer classed with barbers, they were still below physicians.

▼ Lavoisier's greatest contribution to chemistry was his theory of combustion. He proved that this process results from oxygen (which he was first to identify correctly) uniting with other elements. Though his equipment was rough by modern standards, any chemist today would recognize his retort and bell jar.

Retort

Bell jar

Machines and factories

Industry was mainly on a small scale. In the towns there were still master craftsmen (especially in the more skilled trades) who were their own bosses and ran their workshops with one or two employees and apprentices. There were also factories, but they were usually small and ran on water power.

In some countries large industrial enterprises were developed. The iron industry in Russia was one example. Mining depended chiefly on labour – the more miners, the more iron ore or coal produced. Russian iron production increased simply because more iron ore was mined. Techniques changed little.

But in one country, Britain, entirely new economic developments took place in the late 18th century. The British economy possessed all the ingredients for rapid growth, including increasing population, new markets overseas, plenty of money for investment, better transport, the invention of machines to do jobs one hundred times faster than human hands, and – harder to measure – changing ideas and attitudes.

The revolution occurred first in the cotton textile industry, then in iron and steel. As one industry leaped ahead, it stimulated others; one invention led to another; profits created yet bigger profits. This Industrial Revolution eventually transformed western Europe.

▼ Most industry in Europe was still organized on what is called the domestic system. People worked in their own homes, collecting raw material from the employer and delivering the finished article. This kind of industry took place mostly in villages; whole families would take part in spinning yarn.

Coal mining was primitive and dangerous. Polish miners went down the pit in a basket hung from ropes, carrying lighted candles. But mines were seldom dug very deep until the steam pump could be used to prevent flooding.

◄ The spinning jenny, invented in 1764, was a type of spinning wheel which could spin eighty or more threads at a time instead of just one. The immediate result was less work for spinners but more for weavers.

Crime and punishment

Law and justice were in urgent need of reform. In some countries there were so many different courts and so many different legal systems that it was sometimes difficult to know what the law was in a particular case. Many of the courts were run by land-owners or their agents who had little or no legal training.

The law favoured land-owners and the rich. Penalties for crimes like theft or poaching were severe, but the chances of being caught, convicted and hanged were quite small. There were no professional, trained police, and many crimes, such as smuggling and poaching, did not seem criminal to the mass of the people.

People could be imprisoned for debt, a silly practice as a man in prison has less chance of paying his debts. Another punishment for crime was transportation – sending the offender to a convicts' settlement in the colonies. Many of the first settlers in Australia were British convicts.

For people with little to look forward to, there was a great temptation to get drunk and this probably increased crime. 'Drunk for a penny, dead drunk for twopence' said the advertisements for cheap gin. The Russian serf could drown his misery for a few hours with home-made *kvass*, which was made from grain. The upper classes also drank far more than is healthy but at least they could afford good wine.

In coastal regions nearly everyone was involved in smuggling – 'free trade' as the smugglers liked to call it. Other crafts also profited. The main occupation in Alderney, Channel Isles, was making barrels for smuggled brandy.

Hundreds of crimes carried the death penalty, but the law was seldom strictly enforced. When executions did take place, however, crowds came to view the spectacle.

▼ In this prison, a fashionable young lady, fallen on bad times, is forced to work under the eye of a corrupt guard and his wife. They are interested only in collecting bribes from the prisoners.

Better to Work
than Stand thus

The French Revolution

In 1789 France exploded in revolt. The government could no longer run the country efficiently; its debts were enormous, while power lay in the hands of a small group of privileged nobles. The mass of the people were ground down by ancient customs and rising inflation.

A representative assembly, the States General, was summoned, whose middle-class members made themselves into a revolutionary national assembly. A new republican government was later set up.

As a result of the Revolution, the middle class became supreme in the towns, while a few peasants gained land from the old noble estates. More important, the Revolution released the forces of nationalism and liberalism on European politics.

For the first time the state was the nation, not just the ruling class. The French Declaration of the Rights of Man (1789) declared that 'men are born free and equal'. The purpose of government should be to defend the natural rights of man. Governments ruled only as the representatives of the people, to whom power belonged by right.

These aims were not achieved by the Revolution, but they became the ideal for reformers and revolutionaries.

The destruction of the old form of government during the French Revolution was followed by a savage struggle for control of the Revolution by different political groups. Several thousand French people died under the guillotine during the nine months of extremist rule known as the Terror, 1793–94.

Main events

1707 The Act of Union made England and Scotland one country.

1709 Abraham Darby, in England, made coke for smelting iron ore.

1713 The Peace of Utrecht ended the war of the Spanish Succession, bringing a French ruler to the Spanish throne.

1715- The reign of Louis XV (the Sun
1774 King) in France.

1718 The first printed bank notes came into use.

1721 The treaty of Nystadt between Russia and Sweden marked the end of Swedish dominance in northern Europe and the rise of Russia.

1730 Diamonds, hitherto known only from India, were discovered in Brazil.

1733 John Kay patented his flying shuttle, the first of a series of inventions which transformed the cotton textile industry in Britain.

1736 The first successful operation for appendicitis was performed.

1737 Linnaeus published his *Genera Plantarum*.

1751 The first volume of Diderot's Encyclopedia was published.

1756- The Seven Years' War. British
1763 victories secured India and Canada. In Europe, Frederick the Great withstood the combined attack of Austria, France and Russia.

1759 Lisbon, capital of Portugal, was almost destroyed by an earthquake; over 30,000 people were killed.

1760 The Botanic Gardens at Kew, near London, were opened.

1761 John Harrison produced the first successful chronometer.

1762- The reign of Catherine the Great of
1796 Russia.

1765 Watt's improved steam engine was developed.

1768- Captain Cook's first voyage to
1772 Australia and New Zealand.

1769 Nicholas Cugnot, in France, invented a steam carriage.

1772 The first division of Poland, by Austria, Prussia and Russia. After two further divisions (1793 and 1795) all Polish territory was absorbed.

1773- A major revolt of the peasants in
1775 Russia resulted in a closer alliance between Crown and nobility at the expense of the peasants.

1776 The thirteen English colonies in north America issued their Declaration of Independence.

1776 Steam engines were first produced for general sale by the Birmingham firm of Boulton and Watt.

1781 Sir Frederick Herschel discovered the planet Uranus.

1783 The Montgolfier brothers, in France, made the first successful balloon ascent.

1785 The seismograph, an instrument for measuring earthquakes, was invented.

1789 The French Revolution began.

1789 The first cotton textiles factory with machinery driven by steam opened in Manchester.

1790 Lavoisier published a table of chemical elements.

1791 A canal linking the Baltic and the North Sea was opened to shipping.

1792 Gas was first used to provide lighting in houses.

1795 France adopted the metric system of measurement.

1800 Alessandro Volta, in Italy, made the first electric battery.

Famous people

Adam, Robert (1728–92). The greatest of a family of Scottish architects and designers who introduced a new style, based on the style of ancient Greece and Rome.

Bentham, Jeremy (1748–1832). English philosopher, one of the founders of utilitarianism. This taught that all acts should be judged by their effectiveness in causing pleasure or preventing pain.

Catherine II, the Great Empress of Russia (1762–96). German by birth, she became a thorough Russian. She 'wished to do good and strove to introduce happiness, freedom and prosperity'. So she said, but on the whole she failed. However, Russian power increased dramatically during her reign.

D'Anville, J. B. Bourgignon (1697–1782). French geographer and map maker. His maps were the most accurate yet, because he refused to include any geographical feature without firm evidence.

Diderot, Denis (1713–84). French writer and *philosophe*. His great work was his Encyclopedia.

Frederick II, the Great King of Prussia (1740–86). A brilliant ruler who loved the arts yet was the greatest general of the age.

George III King of England (1760–1820) He was the most 'English' monarch for many years and was generally popular.

Joseph II Holy Roman Emperor (1765–90). On gaining full control of Austria in 1780 he introduced many reforms, which failed due to opposition.

Louis XV King of France (1715–74).

Despite many attempts at reform, the state of French finances and the efficiency of administration grew steadily worse. The luxury of the royal court also irritated Louis' increasingly critical subjects. *Après moi, le deluge*, 'After me, the flood' he sighed. It was an accurate forecast: the Revolution broke out fifteen years after his death.

Mozart, Wolfgang Amadeus (1756–91). Despite his early death, the greatest composer in a century of many great musicians. An Austrian, he composed over 600 works, including numerous symphonies and operas.

Rousseau, Jean Jacques (1712–78). French philosopher. Author of articles for Diderot's *Encyclopédie*, he also wrote: *The Social Contract* (1762) in which he put forward the idea that the real authority in the state was 'the general will'; a highly influential book on education; and an autobiography.

Smith, Adam (1723–90). Scottish economist and philosopher. His *Inquiry into . . . the Wealth of Nations* (1776) laid the foundations for the modern study of political economics. He said that the real wealth of the state is labour, not gold, and he supported free trade – no protective customs duties – between countries.

Watt, James (1736–1819). Scottish engineer and inventor. He is remembered chiefly for his improved version of a steam engine, though he made other inventions. He formed a famous industrial firm with Matthew Boulton at the Soho Works, Birmingham, where the word 'horsepower' was first used.

Glossary

economics, economy Terms used to describe the management of the money, products and trade of a community.

Enlightenment A name given to the most important way of thought in the 18th century, which tried to judge everything by reason. It opposed the existing social order and the Church, and supported reforms like ending serfdom and getting rid of the old, unfair taxation system.

guild A local organization of craftsmen or merchants which controlled trade in its area. Guilds usually opposed economic and social change, but their influence was decreasing.

imperial cities Certain German cities which had no overlord except the Holy Roman Emperor. In practice, they were independent.

liberalism The political belief that all men (not yet women!) ought to be free and equal before the law. Liberalism became the dominant political belief in western Europe in the late 19th century, but its roots lay in the Enlightenment.

manor A common form of local community in the Middle Ages, based on the manor house of the lord, with its own law courts and government. This system was becoming rare.

nationalism A political belief that regards the nation, ie, the whole population, as the most important aspect of the state – an uncommon idea before 1789.

patron A rich man (or woman) who acts as protector and perhaps employer of an artist or writer. Few artists could survive without patrons before 1700.

philosophes This means 'intellectuals', a name given to the leaders of French ideas.

physiocrats A group of French writers on economic affairs. They believed in *laissez faire* ('let be'), ie, allowing more freedom to economic forces and to the ambitions of individuals.

Index

60